Courageous

God's Whispers in the Roar of Adversity

Sarah Parkinson

Dedication

This book is dedicated to my family; Chris, Samuel, Keira and Abi. I'm so immensely proud of you and so glad that we get to share life together.

This book is also dedicated to my Mum, whose love of writing and faith in God have given me courage to write and grounded my hope in Christ.

With grateful thanks for all who have encouraged us, and provoked me to write this book, as well as those who've helped us along the way. You are the courage makers we've needed.

Contents

Foreword

In a world awash with Christian self-help, quick-fix, superficial, formulated, even unrealistic approaches to life's painful experiences, people are desperate for authentic support as they face the curveballs that life throws at them. This is where this book excels; Sarah's vulnerable and honest story is a breath of fresh air. Her Bible-based approach anchors her teaching in the Word of God, and the Holy Spirit-inspired concepts she draws out address many of life's challenges in a very practical way.

Sarah helps us to navigate through a life lived on the edge of survival, facing difficulties head on. Along the way she helps us to deepen our faith in Father God's benevolence, love, grace and comfort, always acknowledging His undisputed power and capability whilst trying to make sense of the mystery of life's hurdles and paradoxes.

I have spent time with Sarah and Chris. I know something of the depth of pain, misunderstanding and hopelessness that they have endured. But more so, I recognize the remarkable courage, faith and love that exudes from them. Facing daily struggles, surrendered to and supported by Jesus, they continue living in victory while enduring adversity.

They don't say this of themselves, or have it said of them often, but they are *heroes*. Their lives are a prophetic model to all of us, revealing Christ, the Light of the World, even in the darkest of places.

We all hope and believe for a better day, living in the tension of the now and the not yet. In this place of struggle, we battle to earth the promises of our future in our present reality.

Sarah's book is an invaluable map for the journey.

Clive Corfield

St Albans, England, 2019

Introduction

When you think of the word *courage*, perhaps, like me, your first thoughts are of people who do extraordinary things, those who scale mountains and face huge battles, who endure the lion's den and the fiery furnace, who stand against what's not right and see the impossible taking place. Perhaps you think of mighty moments of courage, ones that feel out of reach for ordinary people like you and me. While courage does include all these things, in truth it starts well within our grasp, in the daily decisions we make. Living a courageous lifestyle lies in the choices you and I make in the here-and-now, the choice not to allow fear to win, the choice to believe better, to hope more, to trust again. Courage isn't just seen in epic moments of victory; it's also witnessed in the small decisions we make in our everyday lives.

I believe God wants us to reimagine the courageous lifestyle as something accessible to all. He wants to fling wide the doors of bravery and invite each one of us on a journey, a journey of courage. It may be that you will take giant leaps forward and make big strides towards the life into which God is calling you. Or perhaps, before the giant steps can be taken, you will take small steps, even just a tiptoe forward.

Courage is not a quality available to a few special chosen ones; it's open to us all.

Courage is not always seen in huge leaps of faith, but in small and almost invisible steps of obedience.

None of us will demonstrate courage by chance. The exceptional decisions to be brave are not something we access from some mystical source; they are formed by our small, daily choices. Today, there is a call to embrace the virtue of courage, a call to step up, to do something, however small. Courage isn't about the size of the decision, but about making the decision - a decision to hope, to believe, and primarily a decision to trust in God.

In this book, we are going to look at Joshua's call to be courageous. In doing so, I want to share with you some stories from our own journey, ones in which we have been called to embrace courage on behalf of our family, to hold on to hope, to cling on to faith, to make a stand against allowing the bad stuff to win. I love the huge moments that come as a result of courage - the lofty moments of awe and wonder, seeing God move before us in miraculous and divine provision - but it's the small moments, the choices in the storm of adversity, that frame and form these big moments.

The Christian life isn't exempt from trial and pain, but when trial and pain come knocking on our door, we can't help but wish them away. For us, they have been, and continue to be, uninvited guests in our home. Our journey has been one of learning in the presence of suffering to trust God no matter

10

what. That's what I mean by courage!

I hope that in hearing some of our story you will feel empowered to take hold of courage, despite the adversity, and that you will find fresh hope, even though you face deserts and battles, so you can meet with the God who has a great plan for your life. The most profound hope in our story has been found in embracing and being embraced by an ever-present God, when it fits my understanding and when it doesn't, and to allow His embrace to lead us on.

As I tell some of our story, I will also include some excerpts from my journal, words I've felt God has whispered into my heart. My prayer is this: as you too stand on the edge of God's promises, as you walk through battles and challenges, that God would whisper into your heart His words, His hope and His courage.

So, today, I invite you to the courageous lifestyle.

Take a glimpse.

You never know what might happen.

1 On the Edge of Courage

After the death of Moses, the servant of the Lord, the Lord said to Joshua son of Nun, Moses' aide: "Moses my servant is dead. Now then, you and all these people, get ready to cross the Jordan River into the land I am about to give to them - to the Israelites. I will give you every place where you set your foot, as I promised Moses. Your territory will extend from the desert to Lebanon, and from the great river, the Euphrates - all the Hittite country - to the Mediterranean Sea in the west. No one will be able to stand against you all the days of your life. As I was with Moses, so I will be with you; I will never leave you nor forsake you."

Joshua 1:1-5 (NIV)

Joshua's Story

There's no other character in the Bible that exemplifies courage more than Joshua. Most people remember the famous words God speaks to him, "Be bold and courageous," and many know about his battles and victories - the walls of Jericho falling down, the parting of the River Jordan, the defeating of the kings of the land God's people are called to occupy, spying out the Promised Land and seeing the fruit more than the giants and the challenges. Joshua epitomises courage. He is a true hero, a pursuer of victory.

However, when looking at characters like Joshua, there is a danger of idealising the moment, sanitising the bravery and imagining a heroism to which we can never attain. We can't do that. When God spoke to Joshua on the edge of the Promised Land, He didn't address the perfect leader, on the cusp of His promises, or someone that didn't require any input, but someone who was the new to the job of leading Israel and who had spent the last forty years in the desert.

Joshua had grown accustomed to the desert, he knew about sand and heat. He had lived in a tent not a palace, and his diet had been a far cry from the banquets of heroes in the making. It had been the same dish morning, afternoon and night - "manna".

I know a bit about manna; in fact, when my children face a dinner that they don't like the look of, they repeat the words of the Israelites, "what is that?" That's a rough translation of the Hebrew, *manna*!

Joshua, on the edge of the Promised Land, and on the verge of walking into the call of God on His life, experienced the same trepidation you and I feel. He knew he faced battles and hardships ahead of him. He'd seen first-hand the challenges of leading the Israelites. It wasn't all glory and wonder - far from it. Leading the Israelites was an ongoing trial, one which must have felt at times like two steps forward and one step back. There were successes, but often failures too. Just when we think the Israelites have understood who God is, they turn again to foreign gods, or created ones, or long to return to their place of slavery again.

As we approach the call of God, we can be in danger of thinking that the victorious Christian life to which we aspire is one free from trial and fear. Then, seeing the obstacles ahead of us, we disqualify ourselves from even starting. We mistakenly believe that the courageous people of God never faced (or face) the things we face.

> **❝**
> The truth is that trial and battle are actually part and parcel of the victorious Christian life

The truth is that trial and battle are actually part and parcel of the victorious Christian life. In fact, without a trial there would be no victory. Without pain there would be nothing to overcome.

When God called Joshua to boldness and courage, that wasn't a call to the absence of battle and conflict. It wasn't a call into a Promised Land where they could simply make themselves at home. If you hear the call of God to do something, understand that there is a battle to come if you are to possess it. The battle doesn't mean that you've missed God; it's a sign that you're right where you should be.

Joshua was called to a land with occupants who had built cities and were none too keen to give them over to a travelling community that had been living in the desert. In fact, in the next seven years that followed this moment, Joshua faced over thirty-one different kings, all of which he needed to defeat.

That's thirty-one battles!

Thirty-one moments when Joshua needed to trust God.

Thirty-one times to exercise his faith in God.

Joshua wasn't told to be strong and courageous because he had it all sorted. God spoke these words to his heart because battles were coming his way. So often we embrace the call to be courageous but then become disheartened and disillusioned in the face of our circumstances, believing we have got it wrong and missed the mark. When life throws us curveballs, things we didn't expect, questions and unanswered prayers, we can be guilty of an assumption that we have somehow missed God's best for our lives. But what if the best of God is found in valleys and deserts? What if our miracles are discovered in the dust and grime of our ordinary, grubby circumstances? What if God wants to meet us in those moments of disappointment when it doesn't look at all as if His supernatural power has won? What if God wants to write in our hearts a story of resurrection, when the graveclothes taunt us that they have had the last word? What if in the face of death, God wants to show us the stone being rolled away? What if the giants that are mocking and undermining us are simply part of the path that God is calling us to tread?

I believe each one of us has heard the Joshua call to be courageous. Maybe today, maybe many years ago, we've stood on the edge of a Promised Land. God's words to be brave and courageous have rung in our ears, but perhaps what lay ahead seemed overwhelming. The brave and courageous Christian life didn't look how you imagined. The lifestyle you hoped would be yours was replaced by some earthy, "normal" living. You stood in the dirt of reality where courage seemed a million miles away.

Perhaps that's exactly how Joshua felt on the cusp of the Promised Land. I wonder whether the joy of adventure filled his heart, or perhaps, like you and me, he felt overwhelmed by the battles ahead of him, perplexed that the promise of God didn't come as a gift to unwrap, but as a fight to be fought.

Our Story

Each one of us has seasons when what lies ahead feels overwhelming and we become stuck, daunted by the future. Maybe you picked up this book because, while you recognise the call to courage, it feels so far from your grasp right now. Perhaps you are in a season where you feel stuck. Life has thrown so much your way and you don't know how to move on or move past. The battles, just like Joshua's, have become relentless and you've lost sight of the Promised Land. In our story, we understand some of that.

Soon after being accepted on the path to ordination, having worked for churches for many years, we went through a tough season. Life became something of a muddle. I felt a bit lost in why we were doing what we were doing. I'd imagined this journey to be an affirmation of God's call on our lives. My expectation was that I would receive some love and recognition from others for what God had begun, but this wasn't our experience; we faced more than our fair share of being misunderstood and misrepresented.

I was so confused. I couldn't understand how we had arrived at where we were. Life felt more like a treadmill than an adventure. Demanding ministry, hectic family life and disappointment about our current circumstances were a constant reality.

In the middle of this season, I became pregnant. Whilst it was a bit of a shock, I looked forward to welcoming a new member to our family. I wondered if this was where we were going to regroup and find our purpose again, taking some time to focus on what God had called us to do. Never did it occur to me that we would face tragedy instead.

Having heard our baby's heartbeat loud and clear at sixteen weeks, when we went for our anomaly scan four weeks later, we both assumed we would see our little baby's heart continuing to beat. However, things took a very different turn. As the staff started the scan, silence fell in the room. There were grim looks, a long pause and then the screen where we should have seen our baby was turned off. We knew what was coming.

"We are sorry, but there is no longer a heartbeat."

With that, we were catapulted into a world of grief for which we had not prepared ourselves. We were ushered back through the waiting room where, moments earlier, we were joking with other expectant parents. Then we were shown into a little room to wait and compose ourselves before we were told what lay ahead. Those days involved blood tests, pills and injections, then times of waiting, just looking in silence at one another, before finally returning to hospital to start a labour I never wanted to endure, to deliver a baby who should have been so full of life, but who would never breathe in this world, while I would be rushed to the operating theatre to help me live.

In all of this, it would feel like death had won. I would never meet my daughter and I would have to prepare for a funeral I had never wanted to arrange.

In those moments, life felt swallowed up. Grief held our lives in a way we never envisaged.

We became stuck.

I became stuck.

I didn't want to move on and let life continue as normal because that would somehow convey the message that death wasn't important. And it was. Very important. We had lost a daughter, a part of our family, so how could we move on?

Had God not seen the struggle we had already faced, the injustice we had already gone through? Were we not already at the limit of what we could handle? How could we move forward when everything felt like it had stopped?

Just weeks before, I had been speaking at a women's conference about the call to courage and those words rang in my ears.

All I wanted to do was hide away.

Those words became a whisper I could not avoid, a persistent echo that I couldn't ignore.

His whisper.

His call not to let the darkness win.

Never had the first little step felt less like courage, but it was.

It took courage - courage to choose life, courage to choose hope, courage to trust His plan for good, that there was a Promised Land that remained for us.

God's Whispers

(from my journal)

Stop for a moment. Drop your burdens, leave them at my feet. I'm not judging you on your results. I'm not judging you on your successes. I'm not. I use people like Jacob. I use people like Moses. I use flawed people to do great things. And I can use you.

I know you feel like you've not got the capacity for all that is to come, but you do. You have. I want you to know that you have what you need. Flawed and incapable makes you dependent on someone outside yourself; it makes you dependent on me.

I want you to know that I understand. I want you to know that I get it. I want you to know that it's ok. Your lack isn't too great for me. I delight to use broken and incapable vessels to do things that others could never do, because I delight to show the world what I can do.

I know you struggle.

I know you feel incomplete.

I know you feel broken.

But I use people just like you.

Your Story

Read again: Joshua 1: 1-5

What are your impressions of Joshua as you read this passage?

Where have you disqualified yourself from being courageous?

What are the battles you can see ahead of you?

Where are the areas you feel stuck?

What are the promises of God that He has spoken despite the battles?

How can you prepare yourself on the cusp of what God has promised you?

2 Digging Foundations

The Lord would speak to Moses face to face,
as one speaks to a friend. Then Moses would
return to the camp, but his young aide
Joshua son of Nun did not leave the tent.

Exodus 33:11

Joshua's Story

Let's track back a bit from the story of Joshua entering the Promised Land, back to where we first meet him. As with Joshua, there is always a preparation process whether you've heard the call to courage many years ago or are new to it all today. This process is found in the everyday life you live, as you position yourself for your future challenges. How we choose to handle ourselves in this present moment will have a profound impact on our tomorrow. All the heroes of the faith, especially the most courageous, dug deep in the season of preparation. Joshua knew the Israelites were on a journey, even when the journey was painfully slow and involved many a detour, but Joshua, whilst waiting in the wings, prepared himself. Every day, when Moses entered the Tent of Meeting and spoke with God, Joshua went with him. Very little is said about Joshua at this stage, except these short words… *"But… Joshua son of Nun did not leave the tent."*

Joshua learnt to be and to remain in the presence of God. The presence of God became the primary object in his field of vision, not the sand of the desert all around him.

It's easy when we've lived in barren seasons for any length of time for our view to be inhibited or reduced and the plans of God to become about survival more than promise. Yet, Joshua held tight to the promises of God even in the desert. He never let go of God's promise to the Israelites. The land he had briefly glimpsed was alive in his memory. At the same time, the focus of Joshua's heart remained the presence of God, despite the dust and mire of forty years of wandering.

Forty years! How easily that reels off the tongue. It almost sounds poetic, until we look at the difficult seasons of our lives that have endured beyond one year and imagine thirty-nine more years of the same.

There is nothing poetic about forty years of wandering in the desert, living in a tent and eating the same food, morning, noon and night! Yet, Joshua positioned himself for the promises of God; he positioned himself for a new land; he chose the presence of God and trusted God for the future.

We know that for any building to be secure it requires strong foundations. The foundations required for a house, will be shallower than those required for a skyscraper. The scale of what God wants to do in us will depend on the foundations we are prepared to build. Building foundations is hard work, it's hidden work. When the building is built, foundations aren't even seen. Yet they are always felt, and for a building to be secure, the work of building foundations is vital. As we stand on the edge of God's promises, are we going to dig deep in the season of preparation to ready ourselves to be able to build for the height of God's promises to us? This foundation digging,

> ...are we going to dig deep in the season of preparation to ready ourselves to build for the height of God's promises to us?

preparation making is a process no character in the Bible was allowed to shortcut.

Abraham had to learn trust and obedience over-and-over again. Noah spent many years building an Ark in preparation to save him and his family in a world where the whole idea of a floating vessel on a body of water was misunderstood, let alone trust and faith in God. David went through years as an outcast, having spears thrown at his head and being hunted and pursued ahead of his promised kingship. These examples teach us that the decisions made before the promises of God are activated are very often far more important than those made once they are being fulfilled.

Daniel knew what it was to embrace the season of preparation prior to him becoming the man of wisdom who interpreted dreams, advised kings and endured the lion's den. He had every excuse to avoid the preparation, to bend and settle for less. He was a captive, a man taken from his home against his will, placed in a foreign land with foreign rules and regulations and gods that he was expected to serve. Daniel knew what it was to feel out of place, to feel misunderstood and unknown. Daniel was invited to serve the king directly, but it wasn't an invitation based on his free will; it was one he dared not refuse. Daniel, best known as the man God protected in the lion's den, knew about courage. He knew what it was to stay true to the promises of God both for himself and for the people he represented. But Daniel's courage didn't miraculously appear in the lion's den; it was fought for and found in his daily decision to pray and to remember what God had spoken to Israel.

Right at the start of his captivity, Daniel decided to remain true to the customs of Israel and to eat according to what God had instructed him. He had every opportunity to compromise, but he didn't. He fought for his right to remain true in the practical matter of his diet and in the spiritual matter of his worship. Every day, Daniel turned towards Israel and prayed even when challenged. He ate according to the custom of Israel and he knelt towards Israel and prayed.

God has a work of preparation in you and me in the unseen places of our lives. This happens when we choose to remain in the presence of God, not to compromise what we believe, and build the habits of our devotion.

Our desert places and our battles will define us. These are the contexts in which we learn to dig deep in the place of preparation. These are the times when we decide what it is, and who it is, we truly stand for.

God has ahead of each one of us a promised destination. His words don't return void (Isaiah 55:11), but in the taking hold of these words, and in waiting for them to be fulfilled, what choices will we make? What decisions will we make to dig deep and focus on the spiritual foundations required? The choices and decision we make are formed in the habits we develop, in what we allow to become our focus and our priority.

How easy it is in the desert place to compromise. Joshua could have joined in with the Israelites' lacklustre following of God's commands, or Daniel with the customs of other exiled people.

Habits of bitterness and disappointment grow so easily in the desert. It takes effort to develop lifestyles of prayer and presence, to take time in God's Word and allow those words to frame our lives, to walk in forgiveness and humility, letting go of offence and choosing grace and love, developing habits of faith and trust and immersing ourselves in the reality of who God is and what God can do.

> **It takes effort to develop lifestyles of prayer and presence**

Perhaps, as you have faced heartache and trouble, you've known what it is for disappointment to become the loudest voice, for the whispers of God to be drowned out by the roar of circumstances, but you have to choose to align yourself with that still small voice that doesn't change.

You may be facing the desert and battles like Joshua, or captivity and lions like Daniel, but there's a strength and resource you can grab hold of, and it's found in the daily choices you make, not letting the gods of the land be your gods, not letting the sand in your face be your vision, choosing instead to look up and spend time in His presence.

Our Story

We had a choice to make in the days that followed our loss. Would we be defined by the circumstances that shouted in our face and the grief that overwhelmed us, the feeling that life had simply been unfair? Or, would we bend to His whisper and His call to courage?

I wish I could tell you that I leapt to courage each day, but rather than a giant leap, it was more like a tiptoe. Those tiptoes of courage and trust started in the decisions I made to open my heart little by little to His love and care. They started with leaving the house, sitting in a coffee shop and opening my Bible and hearing His voice, embracing the Father as I'd always done and allowing Him to embrace me.

Courage for me involved picking up the conversation with the God that I was avoiding, sharing the pain and letting God into my mess - the God who lifts us up out of our mud and mire and sets our feet on the rock (Psalm 40:2).

In the weeks following the loss of our daughter, I had to choose each day to lift my head and look to God. It wasn't that the pain left, or that the grief subsided, but I found in God someone who heard and saw, who didn't wash over our loss, or rush me to healing, but who stood with me in my brokenness and held me as I struggled to put it all together. Life wasn't ok, but the reality was that life hadn't been ok for some time and all the bottled up conversations that I hadn't had with God gradually began to be poured out - the

29

> His whisper became the loudest voice, and my weakness became His strength

disappointments, the frustrations, the questions that I knew had no answer but which I kept on asking, and above all the tears. There were a lot of tears.

Day after day, I sat with God and wrote, wrote the words I couldn't voice, wrote out the sadness I couldn't express, just wrote, and listened. His voice, every day, was what I needed to hear. His whisper became the loudest voice, and my weakness became His strength.

I returned to an old habit of devotion: *journaling*, taking time to write down what was in my heart and then listen and trust the words that returned. These journal entries were and still are moments of clarity to regroup and then reassess what lies ahead.

And so, I listened to His voice in the stillness, in His Word and through my prayers. I had nothing to offer, but only time to give. Sometimes courage is simply stopping, waiting and listening. It's valuing His whisper above the roar of our circumstances. It's recognising that we are not enough but that we've always needed Him. For me, courage in that season was simply standing and telling God I needed Him.

I wish I could sugarcoat that period for you.

I can't.

It was tough.

Every day was tough, but as I faced returning to some normality - or began to accept what felt totally alien as my new normal - God met me. Our loss was part of our story now and was part of who I was, but His words each day resonated in my ears. He wasn't going to 'fix' me and take the pain away, but like the Good Shepherd, God walked with me each day.

I don't have the answers to why we lost our daughter, why we've had to walk the walk we've had to, but I know God sees me and understands, and I encountered His love and kindness every day.

The Christian life is a relationship with an incredibly loving God, who is always present, who calls us to know His supernatural love, who unlocks miracles and signs and wonders, and at the same time a relationship with One who walks with us in trials and suffering.

Jesus travels all the way with us in all of this, knowing first-hand this almost indescribable tension of the divine and the human, the supernatural and suffering, the power and the pain.

I don't know why we lost our baby when God allows others to live, but I do know that He never left our side.

As with Joshua in his season of preparation, my habits of devotion, formed in my season of preparation, became lifelines, moments to breathe again and to be loved. As I opened His Word, through every word I read, I could read my story, my pain and more importantly, I could hear His words and His voice, speaking life to my barren soul.

God's Whispers

(from my journal)

Would you listen to my Word? Would you hear all that I have to say? It's good to come and hear my Word. It's good to come and allow my Word to sharpen and strengthen you. Would you allow me to structure and strengthen your day so that you can accomplish what you need to do? Would you tune your ears to hear what I might want to say through your week?

I know in your life things are jumbled and confused, but if you allow that to dictate your thinking then you too will end up jumbled and confused. I have a rhythm for you to get into, so that what you are walking through doesn't take over and dictate more than it ought to. I want you to know a rhythm and a process, to take time to hear my voice at the start of the week, to take time to know, even when it looks obvious what it is that I am speaking to you to do.

There are times when the prison walls crumble, and like Peter you walk from jail. And there are other times when I want to release the prisoner that didn't even know they were imprisoned. When Saul and Barnabas were imprisoned and their praise brought freedom, they stayed where they were in order to encounter a greater miracle - salvation in prison!

You need "forever" wisdom to know what it is I am pointing to - what it is I am directing you towards. Would you hear my Word in season? Would it guide and direct your days? Would you know that there are times in your day here that you need to stop and just hear my voice and allow me to define your time?

If you're not careful, you will become a blunt tool, just doing whatever is needed to be done, instead of hearing my defined plan and purpose for the day.

You can miss the opportunities that I have ahead of you and for you. Take time to hear my voice. It's not a "nice to have"; it's a necessity.

If you are going to be who I've called you to be, then the time you spend with me will be more than made up for in the productivity that I give you.

Your Story

Read: Exodus 33:11

What daily habits are you making to prepare you for the Promised Land ahead of you?

Do you need to rejig some habits?

How can you do that?

Do you need to start some new habits?

How can you do that?

Have you allowed any habits of bitterness and disappointment to develop in your heart? If they have, take some time to give them over to God, to ask Him to help you start again

How can you make space to linger in the presence of God?

3 When Seasons Change

*After the death of Moses, the servant of
the Lord, the Lord said to Joshua son of Nun, Moses'
aide: "Moses my servant is dead. Now then, you and all
these people, get ready to cross the Jordan River into the
land I am about to give to them - to the Israelites."*

Joshua 1:1-2

Joshua's Story

Joshua had seen his fair share of what God was able to do. He'd seen God's miracles, His provision, His judgements and His mercies. He had served God faithfully under the leadership of Moses. Yet in this moment, on the edge of the Promised Land, God spoke to Joshua. He reminded him that Moses – the Moses who had spoken to Pharaoh, the Moses who had led the Israelites out of Egypt, the Moses who had seen water spout from a rock and food appear from the dew - is dead. This was Joshua's moment to lead the people of Israel. As beloved as Moses had been, it was time to let him go. The season of the desert was over; a new moment was coming when Israel would need to possess that which they had stood on the edge of for so long.

There are moments for each of us when God wants to remind us that He is setting us up for something new. Just as the spring changes to summer, or summer to autumn, the spiritual seasons can change for us too.

There's an intriguing passage in 1 Chronicles 12:32 that talks about the sons of Issachar, men about whom very little is known except that they were renowned for their wisdom; they understood the times and seasons and therefore they knew what to do. What richness of wisdom, to both know the season you are in and consequently how you need to respond! Every season has actions that are specific to that moment. What was required of the Israelites when they lived in the desert would be very different from what was

Every season has actions that are specific to that moment

required of them when they conquered the Promised Land. Whilst habits of devotion will always remain the same, there are actions that need to change in the light of the shifting seasons and times.

It's therefore important for us to recognise the season we are in because with every new season there will be new things to embrace and old things to relinquish, even cherished preconceptions and ideals. We must discern how God wants to move in a new season and how He therefore wants to use us. The methodology of the past might not be the methodology for the present. Furthermore, it might also be very different from what we are going to need in the future.

For Joshua, there had to be a releasing of past methods because he wasn't being asked to lead like Moses. In this new season from wandering to conquering, he was free to lead in the new way that God had called him. There would be things for Joshua to cherish from the desert and things to relinquish. There would be things to remember and learn from, but there would also be new strategies, and the new empowerment to go with them.

We will all face these moments when we are called to receive a new equipping and let go of former things. There's great freedom in knowing that God may give us new ideas and ways to communicate the Gospel. Even though the message remains the same, the vehicles for conveying the message may change. In my life, I've seen how time and time again there come moments when what has always worked just doesn't seem to be working any more. No matter how hard I pray, seek, challenge or rebuke, something has shifted. There has been a moment when the seasons have changed. Like the sons of Issachar, my heart has needed to recognise the new season and know what to do.

There are some season changes that are more bittersweet than others. To say goodbye to a long winter season and embrace the new excitement of spring is a joy. But when people have moved away whom we have cared about, or when things have come to an end that we have held dear, we can wrestle with the change in seasons. As we enter the new, God ends the previous season. When that happens, there can often be a call to let go of things that we've loved and held dear, but in the letting go there's a promise ahead of all that God has for us, knowing that the best is yet to come.

Perhaps for you today courage means letting go of some wonderful things and being ready for the new that lies ahead. Courage means drawing strength from your experiences, remembering what God has done in the past, and holding on to the assurances of what He has been, what will be and knowing that the God who provided in the desert, can provide again. Maybe courage for you means letting go of how you hope God will answer your prayers and how you think God should propel you to the Promised Land and being content just to see what God will do. How often I've heard myself say, "If I were God, then... I would have cut short the desert season. I would have kept Moses alive. I would have defeated the kings before any battles ever had to be fought." But God knows what He is building in you. He knows what needs to happen and He isn't limited to our plans. His plans are so much bigger, and we can trust them because He is good and He is faithful, always.

As you embark on a new season, prepare yourself. God spoke to Joshua next and said, "*Now, you and all these people, get ready...*" God is calling us to get ready. He has promises and plans that are truly wonderful, ones that will fulfil us and enable our hearts to soar. Let's not become disheartened by what we're losing. Let's keep our eyes focused on what is to come.

Our Story

Despite trying to return to normal habits and routines, the grief we walked through was at moments overwhelming. I wanted to rush through the process and get to the other side, where God uses it for good and everything makes sense. We live in a world where we want, in fact we think we *deserve*, everything to make sense. But much as I wanted to accelerate this process, I knew God wanted me to stand and know Him in our suffering.

In this season, God wasn't going to move in the ways I had known Him move before. Having grown up seeing answered prayers and miracles, my Christian heritage is strong; my parents' faith is strong, having walked through many a season of trusting in God. Life hasn't been perfect, and we've faced our fair load of adversity, but we've seen God come through for us. We've seen prayers answered and challenges met. God has provided miraculously for us and comforted us in the trials. God has always been faithful.

There's a great depth to that experience, but there is also a danger that we can become so familiar with the ways of God in the past that we miss His ways in the present. We see the trial and our prayers are to direct God to move in the ways we want and how we believe He should. Much like Jonah, we can get frustrated when our plans for God don't evolve, and we miss how His plans do. There were times when I became frustrated. Couldn't God just deal with the headlines? But I knew in our suffering that God was rebuilding me. Time and again God would speak to me about tall towers and shallow foundations, of trying to build before the foundations had been set.

I knew that God wanted to be in on every part of the process but, as a pastor, I felt embarrassed about the "victorious" Christian life I was demonstrating. I wanted to rush through my grief and get ahead to the part where it was all ok. But I also knew in this unfamiliar season that somehow God wasn't going to shortcut anything and wasn't going to allow me to brush over the big stuff. God wanted to be part of all my life, not just the successful looking parts, but the ugly "shouldn't-see-the-light-of-day" parts.

I didn't want to talk to God about the guilt that had been gnawing away at me since the moment we were told that there was no heartbeat - the "send chills down your spine and stop your heart beating" guilt that engulfed me in the middle of the night.

One question loomed over me time and again. Was I somehow responsible for my baby's death? My role was to bring forth life. Perhaps I'd been so preoccupied with ministry, with family stresses, with my own problems that I hadn't cherished the life within me enough. I'd been pursuing my career and didn't even know my child wasn't living any more.

Guilt was a monster that stormed my brain and I couldn't brush it away. It wasn't that I'd never let God in on my fears, mistakes and failures before, but I knew God wanted to stop me in my tracks. My walk had become about what I did for Him; it was about how I represented Him, it was in my serving and in my work. I had to encounter God in those moments and hear Him reframe my perspective, rewrite my story and turn around my priorities.

My work for Him is still valid and important and a wonderful reflection of something that should always have precedence - my relationship with Him. How God rewrote my experience I don't know, but as I allowed Him into the ugly parts, to the hidden parts, He met me.

I wanted to hold onto that guilt, to let it define me, to disqualify me from the next season, but God just loved me and when it was overwhelming, loved me more.

Perhaps today, as you stand on the edge of your next season, it's not good things you need to let go of, but it's failures in the past. It's unforgiveness and bitterness; it's the ugly stuff you've been trying to conceal. It's that thought that returns that you don't want to relinquish; deep down you know it's holding you back, but letting it go seems to lessen its importance.

Perhaps for you today, courage is letting God take every part of your life, allowing Him to take responsibility and trusting Him more than your own wisdom.

New seasons come and there are always new ways of doing things, new things to learn and old things to relinquish.

God is never limited to our ways, but His ways are higher than our ways, and His mercies are new every morning.

Trust Him!

God's Whispers

(from my journal)

I love you and hold you close. It's such a privilege to walk through valleys with those who cling close and hold on. Well done for clinging close and holding on.

Know that my love meets you. Know that my love embraces you. In the generosity of people's love around you, know me. You are seen. I have seen you. I have seen all that you have walked through, the moments where tough situations have merged on top of each other. I see you. I see how life hasn't been kind. I see you.

I draw close to the suffering heart. I draw close to the pain and heartache. I will not let you walk it alone. I will not let you suffer by yourself. I know things have been hard, but you are not alone. I am close and I reveal my love in the acts of generosity that you see around you. The love and kindness are my ways of drawing close.

Feel my embrace as you wrestle with the mix of emotions and with the darkness and light that your journey encompasses right now. Let my light illuminate you more. Let my love illuminate you more.

I am enough. I have enough for you. You are not meant to walk this walk alone. Walk it with me, and when you walk it with me you will walk it with others. They will emerge and walk alongside you. Walk first with me and I will provide those to stand fully on either side of you, to hold your hands when you are weary. The loneliness you have felt will disappear when you hold hands more with me and I can then provide what you need.

As you make space for me, I make space for you. Right now, I know you are wondering what the catch is and what I will ask of you, but I am not asking of you. Just walk with me. That is all.

Your Story

Read Joshua 1:1-2

What season are you in right now?

In what ways have the last seasons come to an end?

What new things are you meant to embrace?

What are you struggling to let go of?

4 Between Promise and Fulfilment

"I will give you every place where you set your foot, as I promised Moses. Your territory will extend from the desert to Lebanon, and from the great river, the Euphrates - all the Hittite country - to the Mediterranean Sea in the west. No one will be able to stand against you all the days of your life. As I was with Moses, so I will be with you; I will never leave you nor forsake you."

Joshua 1:3-5 (NIV)

Joshua's Story

As Joshua stood on the edge of the Promised Land, God reasserted the promise He'd spoken over-and-over again to the Israelites that the land they were entering was theirs to possess. Every place they walked would be theirs. This sounded great in theory; taking possession of the land was the stuff of dreams! Owning the land and having the right to do with it what you wanted sounded amazing! Experiencing this, well that was a different matter.

A few years ago, we bought a house. Having looked around many houses, honed the possibilities and seen the potential, we went and visited it. The estate agent had an embarrassed look on his face as we met him at the steps. It was what they called a "fixer upper." It had good bones, but not a lot else to commend it. You can imagine his surprise when we phoned and asked if we could go and look around the house for a second time.

Something about the place had caught our imagination. We could see the possibilities. Yes, the odour of tobacco hung in every room, the electrics needed rewiring, the hole in the wall in the bedroom was not an attractive feature, and I try not to remember how the smell in the bathroom clung to the back of your throat, but we chose to see what it could be like and set about the hard work of realising that, staying with friends so we could let the builders in, while we cleaned and painted and scrubbed and cleaned again.

We attacked the house first, and then the garden, both with great gusto. The tangle of brambles and ivy that overflowed in the garden was overwhelming. We would try to tame the weeds only to find them growing again just weeks later.

Possessing a land, much like giving a house an extreme makeover, takes work. It takes hard graft and demands sacrifice, time, effort and sometimes working at the same things again and again.

Here in the Israelites' story, God was promising that when they stepped into what He had for them, there was an ownership and authority that would come simply by being there. God also promised that no one would be able to stand against them - not that people wouldn't try, but that no plan of theirs would succeed.

Perhaps when we read these words, we overlook the obvious; we jump to the place where no plan will succeed and miss the fact that that this doesn't mean that at times people won't stand against us, that at times things won't come our way that try to assert their control over what God wants to do. This is not to frighten you, far from it; their plans will not succeed, so take hope. If you are facing opposition, maybe, just maybe, you are exactly where you should be. So many Christians face opposition and assume that they have missed God's plans for their life, instead of remembering the promise, standing their ground and knowing that no plan against them can succeed.

The verses above show that the greatest promise that God speaks to Joshua is of His presence. God says that He will not leave him nor forsake him. This is the enduring hope of the Christian faith: *God is with us*. It's one of God's names, Emmanuel, meaning "God with us." We so often pad that out into a nice Christmas message and yet forget the reality. God didn't promise that He'd never leave us or forsake us in a sentimental way, perhaps as some suppose. It wasn't the "I'm with you in heart" speech that we've heard and know to be a statement of sentiment not action. This was a strong and definite promise of His presence in the heat of every battle.

Joshua therefore wasn't entering the Promised Land to fight alone. Joshua didn't have the capacity to take hold of this Promised Land on his own. He and his people had the assurance that not only did they have their army fighting for them, but they had the armies of heaven fighting for them too.

They were not alone!

> He and his people had the assurance that not only did they have their army fighting for them, but they had the armies of heaven fighting for them too.

And nor are we.

In 2 Kings 6, a different battle took place between the Arameans and the Israelites. The King of Aram schemed against Israel and no matter what tactic he used, no matter where he camped, Israel was there and seemed to have the upper hand. The King of Aram became irate with his men and accused them of being traitors, but they pointed to another, to a man of God in Israel who told the king of Israel even the very things that took place in the King of Aram's bedroom. The king of

Aram, hearing of this prophet of Israel and how he was responsible for so many failed ploys, changed his tactics. He decided he would destroy the prophet, Elisha, then he could destroy the Israelites.

One morning, Elisha's servant opened the curtains of their residence and looked out to see the King of Aram and his army encamped all around them. They posed a fearful view. The servant fell at the feet of Elisha, and cried out in fear, "What should we do?"

Maybe you know that feeling of being surrounded on every side and besieged. When you wake in the morning and open the curtains of your life, you look at what surrounds you and it's simply overwhelming.

However, Elisha's response was one dependant not on what he saw with his physical eyes, but what he knew with his heart. He responded with calm grace. "Don't be afraid … Those who are with us are more than those who are with them."

Elisha's view was not just framed by what he saw with his eyes but by what he saw according to God's promises, according to who God is. He then prayed for his servant's eyes to be opened. The servant then saw the hills full of horses and chariots of fire ready to fight for them.

Oh, that we would grasp the reality of the presence of God with us! It's not simply a promise of reassurance in the heat of the battle, but of substance and reality. It changes the balance of the fight. It's no longer one man and his servant against the vast army of Aram, but one nation's army against the army of heaven with chariots of fire.

I know whose side I would want to be on!

There is a reality to the promise of God with us, that is far more than we often see. It's far greater than we can imagine.

It's His presence with us that stops the fire from burning us.

It's His presence with us that closes the mouths of the lions.

It's His presence with us that causes the sun to stand still.

It's His presence with us that alters the equation, changes the odds and allows us to secure victory from the jaws of apparent defeat.

Too often we dilute the promises of God in the light of our negative experience. We know that often people have promised to be with us, and the reality of that hasn't amounted to what we had hoped. We project this negative experience of people onto God and His promise to be with us is diluted by our disappointment and lack. God promises His presence in the battle - that's a promise of hope, a promise of possession, a promise of favour – and all these promises will come true.

> *It's His presence with us that alters the equation, changes the odds and allows us to secure victory from the jaws of apparent defeat*

Let's be courageous in the face of opposition and look for the presence of God.

Our Story

As our story continued, and life threw us yet another curveball, one thing we were sure of was God's presence, despite the outward circumstances. In our grief, we didn't know there was more to come our way. My husband Chris had joined the army at seventeen and served for six years. Not long after we had met, he was deployed to Iraq and Afghanistan. Five months after he left the army we were married.

Over the first few years of marriage, I saw a deterioration in Chris' ability to cope in stressful circumstances. I was confused by how such a calm and placid man could flip into such angry rages. I didn't understand and blamed myself. In the confusion of our own tough seasons, perhaps we hadn't paid enough attention to the dark cloud that had appeared.

On the day of our daughter's funeral, we had a call from the Psychologist to confirm Chris' diagnosis – PTSD (post-traumatic stress disorder). We had no idea what it meant, no idea how things would unravel, no idea what that dark cloud would bring. I couldn't concentrate as it was, and assumed a diagnosis was the same as a cure.

How wrong I was!

Over the course of the next eighteen months, I watched, my heart breaking, as my laidback husband disappeared. At first the anger erupted, and we lived in fear of triggering him. Then we began to realize the extent to which he was suffering. The lid that he had shut down so hard to protect us could no longer be kept shut. Aggression was leaking into our home.

As a mum of two young children, on a journey towards ordination, immersed in my own world of grief and guilt, I was bewildered by this turn of events. I found myself holding my family together when all I wanted to do was fall apart. But as the anger lessened, I watched Chris break as he wrestled with the fear and anxiety he had never talked about before. Normal every day parts of life - a family day out, a meal together or even just being in town – became inaccessible. I watched Chris stumbling for words to explain he was afraid in the safest of situations. I realised the extent of his mental illness and that there are no quick and easy fixes.

Many times, people have asked how we have kept going, how we have not fallen apart or given up. It's certainly not that I'm some superstar. There have been moments when I've felt at the end of my tether, but there I have been reminded again of God's promises to us, knowing that God doesn't disappoint or let us down.

In the years preceding this moment, God had spoken so clearly to Chris about becoming a paramedic - a complete career change. This was a huge step of faith which meant leaving behind a well-paid job, studying every evening while working full time, then taking a basic salary to train to become a paramedic. Yet God provided and met our needs miraculously. We had two small children and the tightest of budgets, with no extra money for the "extras" like gifts, clothes, etc. Each month it felt like the figures shouldn't have balanced, but they did. Friends encouraged us and whenever we faced a lack, there was always provision, down to the clothes we needed to dress the kids - even a pair of shoes that I had seen in a shop and couldn't afford. Someone dropped them off at our house without me saying a word. One friend even phoned us and said they had had a pay rise, and they didn't need the extra money, and wanted to give it to us! Every time I worried, or was afraid, God met with us and supplied all our needs. This God who has made straight our path towards Chris becoming a paramedic, how could we not trust Him now that he was qualified?

As we continued to wrestle with Chris' diagnosis and deterioration, God very clearly spoke to me, giving some promises of hope. He spoke to me about His plans for Chris' life - not just for us to endure this journey, but to succeed, and see God's ultimate purposes fulfilled. There are many times when I've felt impatient to see this day, where we have faced moments when God's promises look anything but real, where experts have told us he will not recover, he will not be well, but it's in these very moments when everything looks bleak that God has reasserted His Word to us. God has been so faithful to us along the way; we've seen His hand upon us in the strangest times and places. We have chosen to hold onto God's promises, to believe that God didn't miraculously provide for Chris to become a paramedic, only for him not to be well enough to do his job.

We have chosen in the tough times and in the dark times to hold unswervingly to the knowledge that God is with us. The Christmas card promise of His "Emmanuel" presence is just as real in the tough moments as in the tinsel and baubles.

We take each day as it comes. The journey with PTSD means that you do not know what the day will bring - good moments or dark ones, peace or anxiety, calm or anger - but we do know that in every day we walk, we do so with

God with us.

> We do know that in every day we walk, we do so with God with us.

Right now, we are living in the gap between what God has promised and seeing this come to fulfilment. It's a tough place to live, but like many of you who are doing the same, and like Joshua, it's a time to hold tight to the whispers of His promises, because they remain true and steadfast in a faulty and crooked world. As we wait, God's presence is all we need and it's all you need too. As you hold tight to His presence, you will walk into the authority and ownership that God has promised.

God's Whispers
(from my journal)

Thank you for your trust. Thank you for your hope, for the fact that you keep going in spite of the challenges and the trials. I know there is a lot going on and you feel that much around you is shaken and shaky. Let me hold you still and hold you tight.

You don't have to be afraid. I have a stillness to bring around you even when you feel everything being shaken. Even in that place, I have a stillness I can bring to you, and a calm.

I really do calm the storm. That's who I am. The storm doesn't have to rage around you. You can command the storm to be still. I have not made you to be a victim, I have not made you to be helpless in a raging sea. There is power in standing still, but I have placed within you what you need not just to stand still in the sea, but to calm the seas also.

You are not a victim to that which is taking place in your family. I want you to begin to take control of your family. You hold the keys over your family, and you can begin to call them to their rightful place in the kingdom.

No longer do I want you to be a victim but an overcomer. I am the God of the breakthrough. Circumstances don't have power over you nor do storms define you. You walk with the God who is all powerful and I want you to begin to walk in your God-given authority.

For too long the enemy has told you that you are a victim, that you cannot take control of what controls your life, but that's not who I am and that's not who you are in me. I want you to begin to speak out over your storms the stillness of the kingdom. I want you to begin to say to the giants, "Be gone," and say to the craziness, "Be calm!"

Your Story

Read Joshua 1:3-5

As you reflect upon your life, in what ways have you seen God be with you?

Make a list of God's promises to you.

Where do you see God's presence at work right now?

Perhaps you are facing a difficult circumstance. In this situation, how can you know God with you?

5 Courage, Courage, Courage

"Be strong and courageous, because you will lead these people to inherit the land I swore to their ancestors to give them. Be strong and very courageous. Be careful to obey all the law my servant Moses gave you; do not turn from it to the right or to the left, that you may be successful wherever you go. Keep this Book of the Law always on your lips; meditate on it day and night, so that you may be careful to do everything written in it. Then you will be prosperous and successful. Have I not commanded you? Be strong and courageous. Do not be afraid; do not be discouraged, for the Lord your God will be with you wherever you go."

Joshua 1:6-9 (NIV)

Joshua's Story

In that very moment, standing on the edge of the land that God had promised to the people of Israel, God spoke three times to Joshua these words, *"Be strong and courageous."* If, like me, you are told something once, there's a 50/50 chance you might remember. Being told something twice, I should be getting the hint. But three times! I seriously need to tune in. The problem is, I'm not sure I like the idea of being strong and courageous; it implies battle, adversity and struggle, and no one likes the sound of that.

Somehow in modern society we've come to regard good times in our lives as a sign that God is most present. We've equated settled and peaceful moments with where God has called us to be. We've come to see those exploits that have gone easily and well as the ones that God has directed and blessed. In the process, we have forgotten those Bible stories in which God has led people into adversity, into times of trial, into desert seasons.

Think of Joseph. Even if it was perhaps through his own foolishness and mistakes, he was sold into slavery by his brothers. He was then imprisoned for a crime he didn't commit, in order to put him in a position to save his family in a time of drought and famine.

Think of Jeremiah. He was chosen to speak God's Word to His people in a time of great need. He spoke it faithfully and yet faced ridicule, derision and even had the ignominy and terror of being thrown into a well.

David, a man who was called and anointed to be the king of Israel, who slayed a giant and won many battles against the Philistines, spent years running from Saul and hiding in a cave.

There are so many more such examples that show how we must relinquish this preconception that being a Christian means that we don't have to face anything tough or difficult. It is simply not true that walking with a loving God means a life free from trial, pain and suffering. God does promise us all a pain-free life, but it's not here on this earth but in eternity, where every tear is wiped from our eyes. For now, we are pilgrims in this world, and maybe, just maybe, the battles and the pain we face, rather than telling us that we have got it wrong, reveal that we are exactly where we are meant to be.

Growing up we knew Christmas was coming when my mum would pull out her favourite Christmas album, an old Twila Paris tape. This tape would play on repeat in the home and in the car, in fact wherever we went. These tunes are full of memories and moments we spent together as a family. My favourite song, *Wandering Pilgrim*, tells the tale of the wise men journeying and following the star. It describes their journey as pilgrims on an adventure, needing a Saviour to guide them.

This notion of being a wandering pilgrim in this life, awaiting a heavenly destination is such an apt description of so many of our experiences. Just like the wise men who followed the star, who embarked on a long and arduous journey in the hope that they would meet the King. We too are journeying through this life. The trials and difficulties we face must be eclipsed by the expectation, based on God's promises, that there is a perfect eternity ahead of us. There is a time coming when the old order of things will pass and, as is written in Revelation 21:4, *"He will wipe every tear from their eyes. There will be no more death or mourning or crying or pain."* Being a pilgrim means that we keep an eternal perspective, there is a destination beyond what we can see and know right now, one that is *"a far, far better place"* (Charles Dickens).

Having said that, being a pilgrim isn't a solitary journey; just as Twila's song says, we need someone to escort us, a Saviour to guide us. Our pilgrimage through life requires us to be strong and courageous, to know that in every storm and battle, God is present.

As we look at the journey ahead for Joshua, we see a God of the supernatural, who pulls walls down, who stops the sun from moving, who overcomes every obstacle, breaking through every barrier. A courageous Christian life is one that embraces both the storm and the One who stills the storm, both the desert and the one who heals the barren land, both the trial and the One who is present in the trial. We can have both.

Let's have a high hope today, as you hear God's call on the one hand to be courageous, and as you look at the reality you face on the

> **"**
> *A courageous Christian life is one that embraces both the storm and the One who stills the storm, both the desert and the one who heals the barren land, both the trial and the One who is present in the trial.*

other, just because things look tough, doesn't mean God's not there. Perhaps, if you look closely, it's in those places that you will see God most in action. It's only normal to wish that the promises of God come gift-wrapped straight to our door, that we won't have to face difficulty, that we are removed from obstacles and suffering. This wasn't God's message to Joshua. After all that God had already done for the people of Israel, His message was once again to hold tight, to trust, to depend on Him, to be strong and courageous, strong and courageous, strong and courageous.

Our Story

Many times, over the last few years, I've assumed there must be a point where I will stop facing battles, where I will enter the smooth part of the journey, when everything will settle, everything will be wonderful. I've wanted God to see my faithfulness in the storm and remove it altogether. What I've discovered is that His faithfulness endures through every situation and that when I feel like I've reached my limit, He gives me grace to keep going.

As Chris received his PTSD diagnosis, we then embarked on the journey towards therapy and healing. In many ways, I'm glad I didn't know what this would look like, as I'm not sure my courage would have held, but I guess that's how God works. He asks us for courage to face the next step.

You don't climb a mountain in one go but step by step. The same was true in our walk with the Lord; we had courage to take the first lot of therapy offered, and then the next, and the next, and the next. Many times, it felt as if we had hit a brick wall; Chris would return from weeks away more broken, more afraid, with more coping strategies and grounding techniques. I often wished we had never started this process, and yet I knew we couldn't have continued as we were. Chris tirelessly and relentlessly chose to open his heart and talk about his trauma and learn how to live life better, but the journey was – and still is - very hard.

I remember at one stage, sitting in a room with Chris

and his therapist, listening with tears pouring down my face as I realised that, for Chris, choosing life was a daily decision, that when I would push him to try and come out or go for a run, it wasn't that he didn't want to, but he was afraid of himself and afraid of his own actions, afraid that he wouldn't come home. His courage each day is to choose life and live that as best he can. Mine is to help him keep taking the next step, encourage him to hope and in the dark times hold everything else together so that he doesn't need to carry its weight. I'm not saying we get it all right, far from it. My frustration during this rollercoaster ride can be high and has spilled over many a time, but we know that God has opened the door to the therapy pathways and therefore we choose to use them. From Chris's first appointment with a GP, we've known God's hand opening doors. From that appointment, this GP has supported us and gone far beyond the call of duty on behalf of our family. The initial assessments he had and the way the residential treatment became available were all signs that God was involved. More recently, funding miraculously appeared for some new therapy, meaning Chris didn't have to wait so long for help.

God has been opening doors and we continue to trust Him to open more. While Chris is not perfectly well, we now have more normal days when the cloud lifts, and we are just so thankful. His PTSD scoring is finally coming down; it's not yet normal, but there's progress.

Our journey over the last few years has at times embarrassed me. As a pastor in our church, I've felt my own pressure. Surely bad stuff shouldn't be happening to us like this! I've felt the pressure that we should have achieved a victory that simply eludes us. Yet our walk is not in isolation; many of us face trial and battle. For us to walk this well, we need to hold onto both a theology of the supernatural (of miracles and seeing God's Kingdom reality amongst us), as well as a theology of suffering. Suffering doesn't negate

God's power to work miracles, nor do we deny God's ability to do far more than we could ever ask or imagine just because we are prepared to create a dialogue around the trials and difficulties that we face. I have always believed that God can at any moment heal Chris, and I will continue to pray that we see that happen, but I will not deny God's authority to be Lord in our circumstances and to know Him alongside us as we walk through tough times.

If you are facing difficulty, trial or pain, it doesn't mean that God has left you, but maybe this is the moment to be bold and courageous, bold and courageous, bold and courageous.

God's Whispers

(from my journal)

You don't need to hear new words but remember old ones. I've got it. And one day you will see what I've promised.

I know this feels a million miles away. I know this feels utterly impossible. I know that right now everything in you wants to assume the defeat in order not to be disappointed again, you want to protect yourself, but that is not your inheritance, that is not what I have promised for you. I have promised you success. I have promised you breakthrough. I will make the rough path smooth and I will make a way in the wilderness. I'm not going to let giants destroy you or your family.

The righteous will inherit the kingdom and not darkness. I know that right now you feel that I've undone what you've been building, but I've needed to rejig some foundations. You were building on issues that would have led to a collapse. All that you've gone through and are going through is to re-dig some wells and re-dig some foundations so that you can build well and build right.

My plan is to build the best for the future and not destroy the future. I know right now you would settle for some normal, but I don't even want to let you do that. I've got more for you than that. I'm fixing some things and it'll take a bit of time.

I need you to go slow and keep putting in the right foundations.

Your Story

Read Joshua 1:6-9

What does being a pilgrim mean to you?

Have you at times, seen difficult circumstances as places where God is not present?

How can you change this?

Where can you see God already moving?

6 Courage and Inheritance

"Be strong and courageous, because you will lead these people to inherit the land I swore to their ancestors to give them."

Joshua 1:6

Joshua's Story

God spoke three times to Joshua to be strong and courageous, each one with a different emphasis. This first time He spoke, He talked of being courageous in order to inherit the land. Since the time of Abraham, God had promised His people that they would live in the land that He had set apart. Abraham partially saw this happen, but when Israel and his sons had to leave the Promised Land and live in Egypt, this promise seemed to fade. Yet the promise hadn't died. Indeed, God's promises for you and me never die. What He has called us into remains; though at times it is reframed, it holds fast. As with Joshua, you may find that the promises over your life might well be rooted in words that were spoken over the generations before you.

In this verse, God spoke to Joshua once more about His Promised Land for the people of Israel. His promise to Abraham, Isaac, Jacob, Joseph and Moses still stood; more than that, God now invited Joshua to be a part of it.

As with Joshua, the call of God, when we stand on the edge of its fulfilment, is part of more than we can see. Our story is rooted in what God has already started in generations preceding ours and it stands for those who will follow us. Our decisions to either enter in, or camp on the edge, have repercussions that will last beyond our times.

The concept of inheritance is interesting. By its very nature, inheritance refers to something that belongs to you, something that is a gift from another. It comes not because of your good works, but because another has decided to benefit you. It's a gift like no other because in order to receive it, someone else must die.

Very often an inheritance comes through family or through relationships. When it comes to an inheritance, our role is simply to receive it, to realise it's a gift and take it. The same is true of God's promises for our lives; we don't earn them; they are not given because we deserve them, or because we have worked for it (Galatians 3:18). God's promises are ours to receive; even if at times they may be daunting, they are a gift.

> *Our story is rooted in what God has already started in generations preceding ours and it stands for those who will follow us*

The generational inheritance of blessing is shown so clearly in the life and story of Abram. It is even signified in the changing of name from "exalted father" (Abram) to "father of many nations" (Abraham). Abram's journey to the Promised Land started in another generation when God called his father, Terah. Terah heard God's call to move from where he was living in Ur of the Chaldeans and travel to the Promised Land, and so he started on this journey. However, halfway along he settled in a place called Haran, a place we know little about, other than its name is also the name of his son who tragically died in Ur of the Chaldeans. Coincidence perhaps, but Terah settled in the place of his disappointment;

he settled in the place of his tragedy and grief and never continued towards God's Promised Land.

Years later, God repeated his promise to Abram and called him to receive the land that his father hadn't received. This was not just for him; it was also for Isaac, his yet unknown son of promise. The story of Isaac's miraculous birth wasn't just a story of hope for those since, to whom God has promised children; it's a story about inheritance.

When God calls us on a journey, to enter something new, it can be daunting, even unsettling, uncomfortable and awkward. Abraham felt all these things. Yet as we pursue God's journey for our lives, something is established that is more than just for the here and now; it becomes the place in which the future generation will begin their journey. The story of Abraham, Isaac and Jacob, is a story of inheritance and blessing from one generation to the next. God's blessing comes when we choose to be courageous and move into all that God has promised us.

Returning to Joshua 1:6, God was here reasserting His promise that the Israelites weren't called to live in tents on the edge of their land. In the same way, you and I are not called to camp at the edge of God's promises. Joshua must have felt daunted by the journey because he knew it meant battles, obstacles and trials, but the journey was more than for him, his family or even the nation. The journey was about establishing the Israelites in the land that God had promised to them, so that future generations could remain.

Woven throughout the story of the Bible we see God's promise of an inheritance. We are called sons of God, male and female, because sons are those who inherit. We are called heirs and co-heirs with Christ (Romans 8:17); an inheritance is ours, not because of what we've done, but

74

because of who God is. God calls us to His promises not just for us to feel fulfilled, but so that we can leave a legacy for the generations that we've not yet seen. Many of us know the benefits that came from those who have battled hard to reach their inheritance; we stand on ground that we didn't have to buy. Generations before us fought for our country to be free, fought for the right for women to vote, fought for the right to a free education. As we look ahead, on the cusp of the call to all that God has for us, we need to know that this isn't just about you and me, but about the many to come. Our successes become the ground on which others will stand - others who know God and others who don't. As we follow the call of God, and face the battles all around us, we take hold of territory not just for ourselves, but so that people who follow us can live in our victory.

> God calls us to His promises not just for us to feel fulfilled, but so that we can leave a legacy for the generations that we've not yet seen

Take heart and take courage as you look ahead to God's calling for your life. Your decisions are a legacy and you choose what kind of legacy that will be. Battles will come, more often than we would want, but God's inheritance is a gift, one that needs unwrapping, so be strong and courageous, take heart, there is a land ahead, an inheritance to possess.

Our Story

It would be easy here to take credit for decisions we have made on our journey but I'm acutely aware that our decisions are part of a much bigger picture. Growing up, I'd seen my parents fight to get victory over their mistakes, to change their run of history, instead of allowing things to remain because they had always been that way. My freedom to express my faith how I choose was won by them. My freedom to be who I am was won by them. My freedom to relate well to my family was won by them, and far more than I'm sure I will ever know. Over the years we've had moments when it would have been easy to give up, to admit defeat and allow the problems we face to be part of the legacy we left. But I grew up knowing that my parents contended for our right to express the call of God as we felt led. They taught me how to think beyond myself. I know that defeat is not part of the legacy I want to leave.

The habits of devotion that have held me are habits of devotion I desire to invest in my children. When things are tough we pray together, we talk of the struggle and we hug tight and pray again. As much as I wish I could have protected them from all the trauma, that just has not been possible. This trauma has at times become their trauma, yet even in those dark moments it has been my delight to watch them at their young ages hear the voice of God for themselves and encounter God's love. We ask God to speak to us and we choose together to walk out what we hear.

Some time ago, as we prayed together and asked God to speak to us, my daughter who was 4 at the time, told us that she had received a picture, and the picture was of mountains and clouds. She asked me what it meant. I asked her for more details. She repeated the same words, "Mummy I see a picture of the mountains and the clouds." As I struggled to come up with some meaning, my son, who was then 6 looked at me in bewilderment at my lack of understanding and started to turn the pages of my Bible. He started reading from Exodus where Moses went up the mountain and God's presence came down in a cloud. He started to tell his sister how God wanted to meet with her and that His presence is available to her. He taught me that day, what God wanted to say. It amazes me how much God delights to speak through the generations, that what He deposits in you, He desires to release more in your children.

I have determined that whether life's circumstances are ones I would choose or not, God's blessings are available to us and our choices to engage with them are choices that spill over to the generations that follow.

I can pass on to the next generation the trial and the battle, or I can pass on to the next generation the knowledge of a God who is always loving and present in every trial and battle. The choice is mine.

I can pass on bitterness and resentment or I can pass on forgiveness and grace.

I can pass on regrets for decisions I should have made, or I can pass on stories of adventure and challenge.

These choices are ones that will shape the generations to come. As God spoke to the Israelites in the desert, He again revealed His nature, that He is a God who cannot overlook the sins of three to four generations, but who pours out His love to a thousand generations of those who love Him (Exodus 20:5-6). Your decision to love God and pursue His best for your life will last for one thousand generations.

That's quite a legacy!

Over the last few years, we have been through some difficult moments, moments I would rather have avoided, but as the voice of God has sustained me, so too it will sustain our children. I know as I fight for courage that I'm fighting for more than just myself - for my children and their children and their children's children.

Let me encourage you, in your circumstances and situations, dig deep in the area of your resolutions. You are fighting for a land to dwell in, and that's far bigger than just something for the present moment; it's something to endure generation after generation. God has so much in store for you to live in today and for you to pass on to your children.

One day, following something of a family crisis, I found myself praying over our home. No one else was about and I simply prayed over our beds. I knelt by each pillow and asked God to meet with us, to protect us and guard us and to visit us in our sleep.

The following morning, my son came to me and told me he had had a dream. He told me the dream and spoke of how God had shown His love to him. He cried with me in joy that God had met with him. As he told me this, I remembered the prayers of the night before. Two days later, my son brought me his pillow and held it up to me and asked me to pray over it again. After we had prayed, he carried it back to his bed, taking care in case the prayer fell off!

A legacy was born that day, a legacy far greater than a simple God-appearance in a dream - a legacy of answered prayer, a legacy of belief that God is interested in our sleep as much as He is in our waking moments, a legacy of feeling safe at night with God. I know it's a small moment. When I look at the challenges we faced that day, it was a small answer to prayer. But it was a victory, nevertheless.

When Joshua entered the Promised Land, he didn't conquer it in one moment, one victory or one battle. Joshua saw victory in many battles, but in his lifetime there were still places left to inhabit and land left to conquer. Joshua's legacy wasn't one of a totally conquered land, but of a God who had met them in every battle and trial and would do the same if the people would trust and serve God only.

Every victory we encounter, every answer to prayer we receive, is a legacy we can pass on if only we would trust Him.

History is littered with heroes who held on and endured. Hebrews 11 lists those that believed in the promises of God, though they didn't fully see them come to fruition in their own lifetimes. I have a role as a parent, as someone connected to others, to hold unswervingly to the promises of God, to have an unshakable faith. It's a deposit for those to come.

> I have a role
> ... to hold
> unswervingly
> to the promises
> of God, to have
> an unshakable
> faith. It's a
> deposit for those
> to come

God's Whispers

(from my journal)

I come in the middle of frailty and brokenness to those who know their need of me. I come when you lack, when you need, when you ask. I come to those who know that in themselves they don't have what it takes. You were never meant to have what it takes. You were never meant to be so competent that you didn't need me. You were created for partnership. You were created to work with me. So, when you look at your life and your lack, you are seeing your divine purpose. You are seeing your need to be connected to me.

You are like a piece of the jigsaw puzzle. You are incomplete alone, but you are designed to be connected to me and in that place you will know wholeness.

Never look at your life and your lack and see it as a negative. You were made with that gap because you are created to be connected to me. That lack is part of who you are. It's no lack. It's your strength because it speaks loudly of your need for me. That hole is never empty if you connect yourself to me.

Your Story

Read Joshua 1:6

What does inheritance mean to you?

As you reflect on your life, what things have you spiritually inherited from others and what do you hope to pass onto another generation?

What choices can you make today that will impact the generations to come?

7 Courage and Total Obedience

"Only be strong and very courageous; be careful to do according to all the law which Moses, My servant, commanded you; do not turn from it to the right or to the left, so that you may have success wherever you go. Keep this Book of the Law always on your lips; meditate on it day and night, so that you may be careful to do everything written in it. Then you will be prosperous and successful."

Joshua 1:7-8

Joshua's Story

I'm not sure why obedience is so difficult, and yet it is. From the first time our parents say no to us, to today, obedience seems more of a challenge than a command. It's easy to be half obedient, to *nearly* do all that we are told to do, and yet God is looking for those who will be wholehearted and fully obedient to all that He requires.

This is perhaps why God told Joshua that it takes courage to be fully obedient. As there was for the Israelites, there's a call for us not to turn to the right or the left, but to do exactly as God commands. When full obedience is required, it is so easy to compromise. Somehow, we talk ourselves out of God's instructions; we rationalise according to what seems practical and according to our interpretation of the circumstances. If we are not careful we can skirt on the edge of doing all that God calls us to; we do "most" of it, but not all.

When God called Joshua to be courageous, He meant courage to be completely obedient, not just courage to have a go, or courage to do some of what He wanted. God commanded Joshua to be courageous by obeying *all* the law, doing *everything* that was written in it.

Full obedience isn't something new. In 1 Samuel 15, Samuel the prophet turned to a different leader of the people of Israel, a king who feared the people more than the voice of God. King Saul was asked to destroy the Amalekites - not most of them, not some of them, not just the ones that looked the grizzliest, but *all* of them, to do the job *completely*. Saul heard the instructions and set out, but just a few verses later we see that he chose half-obedience; he *nearly* did what God has asked of him but made a few adjustments that seemed right to him and to the people.

I understand this so well; I know what God has spoken to me but there's such a temptation to adjust it slightly to suit my needs or my requirements. I become one of the *nearly* obedient. But half obedience is no obedience at all. For King Saul, his minor adjustments ultimately cost him his place as King. It cost him his position and his life.

Throughout their journey to the Promised Land, obedience was a big deal for the Israelites, and just a few chapters on from God's call to Joshua, we see obedience yet again put to the test at the battle of Jericho. This was an epic battle, where walls came down at the sound of the trumpets, where there was an amazing and miraculous victory over the enemy, but ahead of that God spoke to Joshua some bizarre and specific instructions about how to defeat a city. It would be easy to imagine that these involved complex battleplans, arrows, hot oil, sieges and hostage taking, yet none of these were included. Nor were decoys, sword fights and battles to the death. Instead, they involved some walking, trumpet playing, not a lot of talking and then, when the moment came, a loud shout in unison.

Joshua and the people of Israel chose obedience, *complete* obedience. They marched around the walls of Jericho, according to the instructions laid out for them, and, at the exact moment God told them to, they gave a big shout and the walls came tumbling down.

Amazing!

Victory out of total obedience!

But there was one last instruction, a simple one, go in and destroy everything. They were not to take anything for themselves. How hard is that? The people of Israel went in and destroyed the city, the people, the cattle, everything. Well, *nearly* everything. They had done all that God has asked them to do. Surely just a little bit of gold and jewellery and Jericho bling wasn't harmful if just one man took a little bit?

When we read this story we may be tempted to think, *how could they do that?* But how easily we struggle with full obedience.

We know God has asked us to invite a list of people to church, surely it's ok if we just invite some of them.

We know God's spoken to us about what we eat, watch, speak or do, but does God really mind if we *nearly* do it all?

Achan, a man from the tribe of Judah, had seen the walls come down. He had heard the instructions, but then he saw a couple of little bits that caught his eye, some small things that surely God wouldn't mind. He grabbed them and buried them under his tent.

Not long after, the people of Israel went out to battle again. They had now seen the walls of Jericho come down and they knew that the town they were fighting was smaller. It should have been an easier battle and they were confident that God had got this. They fought hard, harder than they should, and saw things weren't going their way. Eventually they lost, and not just a small loss. Many people died that weren't meant to die.

Joshua came back to God aghast. "Why did we lose? You said you'd be for us, nothing could be against us, every place my foot touches you would bless." And the truth came out. The wholehearted obedience that God had called them to hadn't happened. Achan's sin was revealed and the half-obedience had to be put right. Ultimately, harsh though it was, he lost his life for this sin. Then the people of Israel went out and won the battle they should have won the first time around.

God is asking us for full obedience, complete adherence to His commands. It requires courage, sometimes serious amounts of courage. If we want to enter all that God has for us, we will need to face the challenge of obedience not just once but many times.

There's an obedience that provokes the blessing of God and that's a wholehearted obedience, one that doesn't compromise on the details, that doesn't change things to suit preferences or practicalities.

> There's an obedience that provokes the blessing of God and that's a wholehearted obedience

I believe being fully obedient to God's voice is often the most courageous thing you or I will do.

In this very clear call to courage, there is also a very clear promise that comes with it: *that you may have success wherever you go... then you will be prosperous and successful.* This is counter-intuitive; so often we compromise obedience to look successful in the eyes of man, to avoid appearing foolish. Yet prosperity and success are the rewards for such obedience. Indeed, when we allow the approval of man to be our mark of success, we succeed less. In a society where success is marked by people's approval and opinion we must be those who are single-minded in our pursuit of obedience.

As God spoke to Joshua, he gave further instruction, *meditate on it [this law] day and night, so that you may be careful to do everything written in it* - an instruction for him to adhere to God's words. This is an instruction for us too, a call to think on and keep reminding ourselves what God has spoken to us.

In order to avoid diluting the words of God to the level of advice which can be taken or left, we need to remind ourselves continually of His words, His Lordship and His position in our lives. As a parent to my small family, I see first-hand my own struggles in the lives of my children, the desire to do things my own way, to be right even when I am wrong, for my rules to overrule all the others and I hear myself as a parent repeating things again and again and reminding my kids that I'm not telling them these things to harm them but to help them succeed. Their battle for obedience is my battle too, a battle to embrace the wisdom and ways of God that don't always make sense and don't always meet the approval of those around me.

Today, let's ask God for that courage.

The courage to be fully obedient.

Our Story

We too have heard the call for total obedience, often in moments where we have already felt stretched. God's words in this season have sometimes been counter-intuitive. My instinct has at times been to bunker down and hide. The nature of PTSD means that you don't know when a crisis is going to hit, you don't know when things are going to suddenly feel out of control, and as much as you learn to anticipate the triggers, look ahead and plan, out of nowhere come struggles and difficulties. Yet the times when I've wanted to hide, avoid the platform at church, retreat to my own company, I've often heard God's nudge to continue and to remain faithful to be and do what He has called me to be and do. In the very middle of some of the hardest times, I've found myself speaking and teaching God's words, and praying and listening with others.

Perhaps you know the feeling of being stretched and you're not sure you can take any more - those moments when you say to God, "If anything else lands in my lap, I'm just not sure I can take it. God I have no spare capacity." It's been my prayer to God regularly over the last few years, "Please God, no more!" And yet, whenever more has come my way, somehow God has given us what we've needed.

Isaiah 54 has been a significant passage in my Christian life. These verses have helped me to grow in faith and to hold onto my faith. They have spoken life to my heart. In verses 2 and 3, God speaks to the barren woman, to the person that is standing in the gap between where God has called her to be and where she is right now. God tells her to stretch wide her tent curtains, lengthen her cords and strengthen her stakes. As I read these verses afresh in this season, I suddenly understood in a new way "the stretch" involved in total obedience. We want to grow to all that God has called us to, but we struggle with this feeling of stretch. Sometimes situations are going to come into our life that "feel" like a stretch, that "feel" outside of our capacity, and yet God is building in us an ability to handle more.

This is not to say that we say yes to everything and get ourselves burnt out, far from it, but there may be moments of obedience where everything in us feels maxed out and God asks us to take another step. That's a kingdom stretch, where we surrender our right to be comfortable, and lean into His right to grow us to His capacity.

A few years ago, I was approached in the playground about becoming a school governor. I had registered some interest at the start of my son's time in the school and thought nothing more about it. My intention was to politely turn it down, but I promised to take the information home and look at it. As I prayed, I told God all the reasons why this was a bad time and how life was full. However, I clearly sensed God asking me, "Is there any other reason why you would turn this down, other than the fact that your life feels full?" I had thought that was a good reason; I was trying to be wise with my time and not over-commit to things, and yet every time I determined to say no, God's question would return to me. I even tried a different approach. "God, I work for you and serve your church. Surely that is enough." But His question returned! Was I going to assert my right to say no, or allow myself to feel stretched to be obedient? I said yes with some trepidation.

Since then, I have often found myself feeling out of

my comfort zone, not least struggling to understand the many acronyms in the educational world, but strangely my hours have somehow stretched; the extra evenings out have worked. I've been able to serve the school community for the season and have a voice there. It's been a privilege to be able to grow some new skills and learn how to operate in a different arena.

For us, we've faced many moments of obedience. There have been situations where I've had to say no and put family ahead of everything else, but at other times there have been counter-intuitive moments, when God has asked me to step up and speak out, to give my time to others, when I've felt I've had little enough to hold onto myself. The times when I've wanted to say no, to let rip on how tough things are and to feel sorry for myself, have been some of the moments when I've felt the most blessed in saying yes. The issue isn't about my capacity, it's about God's, and it's not about how I feel, it's about what He says.

My feelings are a good indicator of how my heart is responding to circumstances, but they are not the most reliable factor in responding to what God is saying. Sometimes God wants to do something despite my feelings, just because of who He is.

> **The issue isn't about my capacity, it's about God's**

Obedience is a challenge we all face, and a choice we daily make. I think right now of some areas where I know God is asking me not to compromise and to work hard, and my choice must be to say yes to His call. Obedience is about trust and allowing God to be in control - completely in control. Obedience is wholehearted; it doesn't compromise, it's tough, but imagine what we might encounter on the other side of obeying God.

God's Whispers

(from my journal)

Don't let go of the future that I have for you. It's not a little future. It's not a minor detail. I have a future for you and despite the captivity of today, it's one with a hope and a joy. I will take your test and turn it into a testimony. I will take your difficulty and turn it into a destiny. I will cause the words you speak to not just sound, but to resound.

You are called to have a voice that is bigger and deeper and that will echo into eternity. Hold tight, don't be afraid. I've not forgotten my plan for you. I will hold you into the future. Keep on keeping on... I am proud as proud can be of you. I'm not disappointed. I am for you, not against you. Don't let go or give up. Hold tight and hold firm.

Your Story

Read Joshua 1:7

In what ways do you struggle with obedience?

Can you think of times when you haven't been fully obedient to what God has asked you to do?

Are there any things right now that God is asking you to do that you are struggling to do?

Spend some time asking God for courage to be fully obedient to all that He wants from you.

8 Courage in the Face of Fear

"Have I not commanded you? Be strong and courageous! Do not tremble or be dismayed, for the Lord your God is with you wherever you go."

Joshua 1:8

Joshua's Story

God repeated His command to be strong and courageous a third and final time. He told Joshua to have courage in the face of fear as the Israelites embarked on the journey He had called them, to possess the Promised Land, a land which Joshua had seen forty years before when he spied it out, a land he knew was full of good things in abundance, a land that flowed with milk and honey (Numbers 13:27) and had the kind of fruit Marks and Spencer would be proud of, but a land that also contained giants.

There were twelve spies that infiltrated the Promised Land including Joshua. All twelve had seen the territory God had planned for them and were called to tell all of Israel about the provision, the produce and the possibilities. However, for ten of these spies, all they could see were the giants who loomed on the horizon - the strong descendants of Anak who were much feared. The people chose to dwell on these negative reports and had to live through forty years of wandering in the desert, awaiting a time despite the fear, to enter the Promised Land.

> **The call of God sometimes comes to the places where we feel afraid, to confront the giants we've been avoiding**

The call of God sometimes comes to the places where we feel afraid, to confront the giants we've been avoiding. When we are on the cusp of something new in God, it is natural to be afraid. However, fear needs to be overcome because so often it causes us to say no, to retreat and hide. Just like the ten spies, it causes us to miss out on what we could have enjoyed, to delay the promises of God. Fear's role very often is to lead us to a place of inaction, where we would rather maintain the status quo than risk what we know. Fear causes us to stand still. When you look over the regrets of your life, broadly speaking they will fall either into regrets of action (things you have done) or inaction (when you've had the opportunity to do something and you haven't). Psychologists tell us that in the spur of the moment we can often regret our actions, but when people reflect upon the whole course of their lives, the greater regrets are those of inaction, where we could have done something and didn't because of fear. Fear's role is to hold you in a place of inaction.

Fear has this strange ability to sound like wisdom, like the voice of reason and common sense. We readily agree to this wisdom because it tells us to avoid the big, scary things in life. However, when we draw back because of fear, we don't consider the cost of our disobedience. As in the case of the ten frightened spies, fear masks the opportunity and causes us to stay where we are, not to try something new. We can at times be at fault because we hold this mistaken belief that the will of God is the ultimate downy pillow where we lay our head. This isn't the what the heroes of the Bible experienced. For them, being in the will of God often meant breaking out of their comfort zones. Today we want the feel-good factor. We want a fear-free life. We don't realise that total obedience does not eradicate fear. It causes us to know that God is with us even in the face of fear.

Fear is no stranger to the great men and women of the Bible. When David the boy shepherd approached the army of Israel, he discovered an entire nation paralysed by fear (1 Samuel 17). They were stuck there because of a giant. This giant, Goliath, would parade in front of them, reminding them what they did not have and shouting about his own size and ability.

I find it interesting to read what Goliath said and what David repeated. Goliath in his daily chant "defies the armies of Israel…" Goliath was calling into question the Israelites' right to the land and their ability to fight. What David heard was subtly different. He asked, "Who is this uncircumcised Philistine that he should defy the armies of the living God?" David wasn't afraid, because he knew that Goliath had missed the point. In defying the Israelites, Goliath was also defying the "living God." That immediately put him on the losing side.

We will all face giants at times, things that could cause us to tremble and be afraid. These figurative giants remind us of our weakness and frailty. They shout of their qualifications and our lack. They call into question our right to possess the Promised Land.

A giant's ability to keep you where you are is based on you not understanding that when it defies you, it also defies God's promise to you. Don't let's forget that we do not fight alone but we stand alongside the armies (more than one) of the Living God. Fear had held the Israelites captive; they had become stuck, listening to Goliath's chant every day for forty days, afraid to act. The solution wasn't greater weaponry; a stone and sling were all that was needed. It wasn't in greater numbers; one boy took to the field of battle. It wasn't in a more experienced soldier; David had no military record. The solution was in a change of perspective.

Fear will come and whisper in our ears and sometimes it will roar in our faces but if we could just hold onto who God is, that He is not just a God of the past, but a living God who is present in our present, and whose love for us is tangible, fear will not be able to remain. The Bible is clear, "Perfect love casts out fear" (1 John 4:18). God's perfect love for us isn't remote and hard for us to access; it's open to every heart that welcomes Him close. The truth we know and hold onto is that Jesus came into this world as a tangible expression of the Father's love, to make a way so that each one of us can know Him, feel Him and encounter His love. All we need to do is to take hold of it.

Perhaps like me, it's all too easy to listen to fear's voice. It's been the standard accompaniment to life because it can sound so easily like the voice of reason and sense. "Don't try again, you might get hurt." "Don't risk, it might go wrong." As you follow the wisdom of fear you may at first feel peace, but panic will soon set in should you decide to ignore its decree.

Here's a truth it has taken me some time to understand, God will never guide us according to fear. When asking for God's counsel, fear of getting it wrong, making a mistake, disappointing others, will not be God's voice. How do I know this to be true? Fear and love are total opposites and God is love, therefore He cannot be fear. There is a wisdom higher than fear, and this is a wisdom of love. His love causes us to act.

As we embark on the call of God, perhaps you will need to draw a line in the sand, saying no to fear, and no to fear being your guide. God has a different kind of guidance, the wisdom of love. Sometimes this will come in the face of our fear.

> There is a wisdom higher than fear, and this is a wisdom of love

Like Joshua, let's take hold of some courage, believing that God who doesn't leave or forsake us. He is with us wherever we go.

Our Story

Fear has been something of a constant companion in my life - fear of disappointing others, of making mistakes, of looking foolish and getting things wrong. I've lost count of the hours of sleep that have been lost to the voice of fear. In our early marriage, many times as I sat under the weight of fear, it has been Chris who has held us together and kept us fixed on God's will and priority, yet as PTSD took a hold of Chris, I saw in Chris the fear I myself had battled.

As we've let people know parts of our journey, often my friends without faith will ask, "How can you still believe in God, given your circumstances?" For me the answer is, "I'm not sure how I could have gone on this journey without God."

Something changed in me in the months following the loss of our daughter that it's only now I am beginning to see. I was at my lowest ebb. I couldn't function or do anything. I felt overwrought by guilt. I knew I was letting people down. I felt the sting of failure and I was walking in the fear I had always avoided. In my understanding, God should have been distant, but His voice was the clearest I've ever known. God was not just present, but personal - listening, speaking and loving my fractured heart. I could do nothing to earn it and yet I was embraced by His love, a perfect love, that casts out fear.

Jesus told a parable about a shepherd who lost one sheep and left the ninety-nine to go after it. When he found it, he rejoiced. This familiar parable has somehow always been associated for me with Jesus going after those who don't know Him, or have fallen away from His plan, yet in this season, I came to realise that it is a parable of how God loves each of us. We each are the one after whom God will chase, for whom God will fight, for whom God will change His priorities. This parable is an expression of the lengths God will go to show everyone His love, His love that dispels fear.

Following the loss of our daughter, fear's voice was loud, telling me to be grateful for the family we had, to accept our family as complete despite the sense that it wasn't. As we rationalised and wrestled, we couldn't shake the desire for another part of our family and we prayed often that God would only grant us an answer to this in His time and in His way, that our foolishness wouldn't lead us any way that He hadn't gone ahead of us.

Eight months after our miscarriage, we found out that I had become pregnant again. Pregnancy changes following a miscarriage and this time it was a very different experience; fear was never far away. Time and time again I had to carry my fear to the Lord and ask Him to calm the storm going on in my heart, yet with this pregnancy God's voice grew. God's promises just resonated in a new way.

Abigail Hope was born on the 12th March 2018, beautiful, healthy and well. Her name is a declaration of God's promises to us. Abigail means "father's joy" - God's promise that one day PTSD will be gone, that He has promised all of our family joy.

And *Hope,* because there is always hope following God.

The courageous lifestyle isn't devoid of fear, but it's not letting fear win. I still hear fear roaring its ugly chants at me, telling me I'm no good, telling me I can't do it, telling me things will never change, but I know fear's roar misses out the truth that I'm surrounded by the armies of the living God. I know too that God loves me perfectly, even when I am not perfect.

Today, let His perfect love meet you in your fear, and let love's whispers silence the shouts of the giants, so that you know all of God's promises are yes and amen (2 Corinthians 1:20).

God's Whispers

(from my journal)

I hear you. I know the waves of this storm are high. They are at their peak. They are shouting of the strength of man and the strength of failure. They are declaring that life cannot be found, and hope is wasted. But that's not my shout and that's not my whisper. My whisper is still that I am good. My whisper is still that I can do all things. My whisper is still that no matter what weapon formed against you tries to rear its ugly head, it cannot and will not prosper.

I know right now it feels dark and tough and hopeless and the end of a road, but it absolutely is not and if you keep listening to my whisper, I will walk you on the path that I've ordained for you.

I know the storm is tough. I know that your strength is being questioned, but don't fear. DO NOT fear. This is not your lot forever. This is not your portion. I am still the God of my word and I will not fail you.

I will not forsake you.

Your Story

Read Joshua 1:8

In what areas are you struggling with fear?

What is God's truth to you in the face of your fear?

Spend some time today reflecting on the Father's love for you.

Epilogue

So, here's your part, where we turn this over to you, to your story. Joshua's story is one of courage, of adventure, but also of battle. His story is drafted in the land of wandering, in deserts and dust, in failure, but it's completed in obedience, in faithfully following God's directions and steadfastly holding to His promises.

You might find yourself in the vast sand dunes of discouragement, or the forgotten valleys of unanswered prayers, but it's your choice from here whether you allow the disappointment to dis-appoint you from the future God's written for you. God didn't promise Joshua that it would be easy. He didn't promise Him a skirmish-free path to the Promised Land, but He promised Joshua and all God-followers through the ages - including us today - that He is with us. He will never, no not ever, leave us nor forsake us. God's not in the business of abandonment or giving up, whether you find yourself in the miry clay or the deepest pit.

His promise of His presence is present today.

The courageous lifestyle isn't just for kings, heroes and those with a special call; it's available to all - to shepherds, those with no weapons to fight, those hiding in the winepresses of life, those whose voice is ignored, whose words aren't heard. It's available to the old and the young.

It's available to you.

Our incomplete story is written to offer you a hand of comfort, companionship and courage, that you might know you're not alone.

Don't give up on the journey.

Don't give up in the battle and the fight.

Don't walk away.

His promises remain firm and true.

There's hope in the journey, in this pilgrimage we walk.

So then, take a deep breath, a ginormous gulp of fresh air, and remember there's a Promised Land for you to inherit. It's there for you, even in the battle, even in the trial.

Take courage, dear one. This book was written for you, so that you would hold tight in the battle.

Look up to the One who is with you right now.

God's still small voice is available for you.

His love is close.

Whether you know the storm, the battle or the desert, it's time to take courage.

Now it's your turn to write your own story.

Yet God

In the darkest night and hardest day… yet God.
When the enemies flood blocks out the way… yet God
When the world seems like it's upside down
and the evil's taunt is the loudest renown – yet God.

There is no shout that will block the sound,
the whisper of God will still surround
When the waves are high and the storm pounds deep,
the love of God rocks my soul to sleep

I will not fear at the taunts I hear,
in the hardest place, my God is near.
No matter who declares they've won
I will lift my eyes to the Son

For in every place my soul will tread… yet God
No matter the voices in my head… yet God
The fear can roar, the wind can blow,
But the love of God, is the truth I know

For no matter what my eyes can see
The empty grave holds the victory
That tells the story of a higher power
The place I run is a strong tower

There is no height, or breadth too deep
That the love of God can not reach
His love that turns wrong things right
Will be my view and my might

Yet God.

Sarah Parkinson 2019

Note: Ahead of publishing this book as intended we found ourselves navigating another difficult chapter of our lives, needing to run afresh to God's wisdom, love and grace. I wrote this poem early into this season, as a statement of fact. It's truth. No matter what is going on in your life, God's words hold true and God's truth will win. My prayer for you as you read this book, is that you will encounter this reality – yet for God.

About the Author

Sarah Parkinson is a pastor and part of the team at Letchworth Garden City Church with a passion to teach, equip and journey alongside other people. She is married to Chris, and has three children; Samuel, Keira and Abigail.

www.sarah-parkinson.com

Printed in Poland
by Amazon Fulfillment
Poland Sp. z o.o., Wrocław

61314182R00063